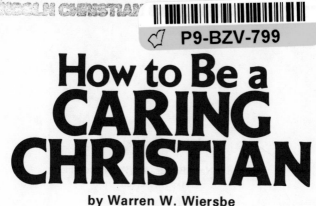

How to Be a
CARING
CHRISTIAN

by Warren W. Wiersbe
General Director
Back to the Bible

Back to the Bible

Lincoln, Nebraska 68501

114,000 printed to date—1988
(5-5970—3M—18)
ISBN 0-8474-6503-9

Printed in the United States of America

Contents

Chapter   **Page**

1. Love One Another 5
2. Wash One Another's Feet 12
3. Receive One Another 20
4. Edify One Another 28
5. Do Not Judge One Another 36
6. Bear One Another's Burdens 44
7. Serve One Another 53
8. Forgive One Another 61
9. Submit to One Another 69
10. Prefer One Another 77
11. Show Hospitality to One Another 85
12. Lie Not to One Another 93

Contents

Chapter   Page

1. Love One Another
2. Wash One Another's Feet 12
3. Receive One Another 20
4. Edify One Another
5. Do Not Judge One Another
6. Bear One Another's Burdens
7. ... One Another
8. Serve One Another
9. Submit to One Another
10. Prefer One Another
11. Show Hospitality to One Another 65
12. ... One Another 79

Chapter 1

Love One Another

How important it is for you and me as God's people to make an impact on this world in which we are living. This begins with a right relationship with God and a right relationship with one another. I suppose one of the biggest misunderstandings we have about the Christian life is thinking that we can get along with God and not get along with each other. But that is a lie; it is impossible to love God if you hate your brother. We are going to study the "one another" statements in the New Testament because they tell us in a practical way *how* to love one another.

If you will check your concordance and your New Testament, you will find 12 different references that contain these words: "Love one another." There are many other references in the Bible about Christian love, but in this study I want to emphasize the statements that tell us to "love one another."

God's Commandment

The first statement is in John 13:34,35. Our Lord Jesus, before He went to Calvary, said to His disciples, "A new commandment I give unto you, That ye love one another; as I have loved you, that ye also love one another. By this shall all men know that ye are my disciples, if ye have love one to another." He repeated that statement in John 15:12: "This is my commandment, That ye love one another, as I have loved you." He repeated it again in John 15:17: "These things I command you, that ye love one another."

Is it right for God to command us to love one another? Let's imagine a young man—perhaps he is on a Christian college campus somewhere—who sees a young lady and falls in love with her. But she is not the least bit interested in him! So he goes up to her and says, "I command you to love me!" Can a man do that to a young lady? Of course not! Then how can God command *us* to love one another?

We must understand that Christian love is not an emotional feeling that we manufacture. Christian love means this: We treat each other the way God treats us. Christian love is not a matter of feeling, it's a matter of willing. "God so loved . . . that he gave" (3:16). God's love was not a sentimental feeling. God's love expressed itself in action. Christian love is an act of the will—we *will* to treat each other the way God treats us.

How does God treat us? God forgives us, so we forgive one another. God is kind to us, and so we are kind to one another. God receives us, and so we receive one another. We may not have the same personalities, or we might not even have the same interests, but we willingly and deliberately treat each other the way God treats us. This is what it means to love one another.

6

I'm going to have a difficult time washing your feet if I don't love you. I'm going to have a difficult time forgiving you if I don't love you. The interesting thing is this: The more we deliberately will to love one another, the more our feelings begin to change; and lo and behold, we even start to *like* one another!

You might not want to spend a week's vacation with some Christians, but you can still treat them the way God treats you. As we love one another more and more, we learn to like one another. We can get along with one another to the glory of God. So the first reason we should love one another is *because God commands it*. Jesus Christ has every right to command us because He has revealed His love to us. He said, "Greater love hath no man than this, that a man lay down his life for his friends" (John 15:13). But He laid down His life for His enemies! (see Rom. 5:8,10). He gave us the perfect example of love by His life and by His death.

God's Law

This commandment to love one another is repeated in Romans 13:8. Paul was discussing in this chapter our relationship to government and to the law. "Owe no man any thing, but to love one another: for he that loveth another hath fulfilled the law." The Old Testament Jew had many laws to keep—laws that governed the land, laws concerning his relationship to property and his neighbor, laws about the tabernacle and the sacrifices. But Paul said that, for the New Testament Christian,

7

one commandment takes care of all the regulations. If I love you, I'm not going to try to kill you. If I love you, I'm not going to steal from you. If I love you, I'm not going to bear false witness against you.

The moral law of God still stands. The righteousness of God's law is still required. However, we do not obey the law from external fear; we obey the law from internal love. It is not compulsion on the outside; it is compassion on the inside. We love one another and this love takes care of all the commandments that God gave in the law.

Love is not a substitute for the law. For me to say "I love you, and that takes care of it!" does not really take care of it. Love helps us to fulfill the law. Love is the motivation for obedience.

God's Teaching

In I Thessalonians 3:12 we find another reference to loving one another. Paul was praying for the Thessalonian Christians: "And the Lord make you to increase and abound in love one toward another, and toward all men, even as we do toward you." There is always room for more love. He repeated this theme in I Thessalonians 4:9: "But as touching brotherly love ye need not that I write unto you: for ye yourselves are taught of God to love one another." God the Father has taught us to love one another by giving His Son. God the Son has taught us to love one another by giving His life. And God the Holy Spirit, who lives within us, teaches us to love one another. Romans 5:5 states, "The love of

God is shed abroad in our hearts by the Holy Ghost [Spirit] which is given unto us."

We love one another because Jesus commands us to, and we love one another because this is the fulfillment of God's law. We also love one another because we have been taught of God to love one another. In fact, the great evidence of Christian discipleship is love. Jesus said, "By this shall all men know that ye are my disciples, if ye have love one to another" (John 13:35). What marks a true Christian? Carrying a Bible? Anyone can carry a Bible. Singing a hymn? Anyone can sing a hymn. Going to a church service? Anyone can do that. What is it that identifies true Christians? They love one another. We love because we are taught of God to love one another.

God's Nature

In I Peter 1:22,23 the apostle said that we should love one another because this is a part of our new birth: "Seeing ye have purified your souls in obeying the truth through the Spirit unto unfeigned love of the brethren, see that ye love one another with a pure heart fervently: being born again." The new nature of God within us gives us the power to love.

My old nature is not very loving; it loves the things that are wrong. Paul wrote in Titus 3:3 that once we were "hateful, and hating one another." But when you are born again and you receive that wonderful new nature of God, love moves in. Do you know why? "God is love" (I John 4:8). Since God is love

9

and God is my Father, then I share my Father's nature. So I should experience love, and I should share love.

First Peter 1:22 states that this love should be "unfeigned." That means sincere, not artificial. Some people gush all over us because they want us to think that they love us, but it is only so much talk. Unfeigned love means sincere love, fervent love— "with a pure heart fervently" (v. 22). That "pure heart" is important. If my heart is not pure, it means there is sin in my heart. If there is sin in my heart, I really cannot love you because sin is basically selfishness. If there is going to be fervent love from my heart, my heart has to be pure.

Here then are three characteristics of Christian love: unfeigned (sincere), pure and fervent. The word "fervent" describes the striving of an athlete. The kind of energy that an athlete puts into winning the game, we should put into loving one another. I wonder if we are as energetic about our love as we are about our tennis, our baseball or our bowling?

In I John there are five verses that say, "Love one another." We read in I John 3:11: "For this is the message that ye heard from the beginning, that we should love one another." This statement relates to verse 10: If we are the children of God, we are going to love one another. We read in I John 3:23: "And this is his commandment, That we should believe on the name of his Son Jesus Christ, and love one another, as he gave us commandment." First John 4:7,8 says, "Beloved, let us love one another: for love is of God; and every one that loveth is born of

God, and knoweth God. He that loveth not knoweth not God; for God is love."

God commands us to love. Then He puts within us His own nature to enable us to love one another. The new birth creates within us a desire to love God and to love others. First John 4:11,12 states, "Beloved, if God so loved us, we ought also to love one another. No man hath seen God at any time. If we love one another, God dwelleth in us, and his love is perfected in us." That is an interesting statement. Nobody can see God, but they can see God's children. And if God's children are loving one another, then the world will know how wonderful it is to know God. The tragedy is that often the world looks at God's people and cannot see that they love one another. I fear sometimes the world looks at us and says, "Look how they disagree with one another! Look how they fight one another!"

Our last reference is in II John 1:5: "And now I beseech thee, lady, not as though I wrote a new commandment unto thee, but that which we had from the beginning, that we love one another." From start to finish, it is "love one another."

These 12 passages refer to the same wonderful privilege—the privilege we have of loving one another. But all of this has to be practiced. If we love one another, we are going to treat one another the way God treats us. This means forgiving one another, being kind to one another, seeking to build up one another. As we study the "one another" statements, we will see how practical Christian love can be.

Chapter 2

Wash One Another's Feet

Caring Christians love one another.

This love is not a feeling they manufacture. God puts this love within their hearts. It is the work of the Holy Spirit as they yield to Him.

But loving one another is a very practical thing. It is not a matter of words only; it is a matter of deeds. It is one thing to say to someone, "I love you" but quite something else to prove it by your actions. This is why we are studying the "one another" statements in the New Testament. One evidence of Christian love is our willingness to wash one another's feet.

"Now before the feast of the passover, when Jesus knew that his hour was come that he should depart out of this world unto the Father, having loved his own which were in the world, he loved them unto the end. And supper being ended, the devil having now put into the heart of Judas Iscariot, Simon's son, to betray him; Jesus knowing that the Father had given all things into his hands, and that he was come from God, and went to God; he riseth from supper, and laid aside his garments; and took a towel, and girded himself. After that he poureth water into a bason, and began to wash the disciples' feet, and to wipe them with the towel wherewith he was girded. Then cometh he to Simon Peter: and Peter saith unto him, Lord, dost thou wash my feet? Jesus answered and said unto him, What I do thou knowest not now; but thou shalt know hereafter. Peter saith unto him, Thou shalt never wash my feet. Jesus answered him, If I wash thee not, thou hast no part with me. Simon Peter saith unto him, Lord, not my feet only, but also my hands and my head. Jesus saith to him, He that is washed [all over] needeth not save to wash his feet, but is clean every whit [entirely]: and ye are clean, but not all. For he knew who should betray him; therefore said he, Ye are not all clean. So after he had washed their feet, and had taken his garments, and was set down again, he said unto them, Know ye what I have done to you? Ye call me Master and Lord: and ye say well; for so I am. If I then, your Lord and Master, have washed your feet; ye also ought to wash one another's feet. For I have given you an example, that ye should do as I have done to you. Verily, verily, I say unto you, The servant is not greater than his lord; neither he that is sent greater than he that sent him. If ye know these things, happy are ye if ye do them" (John 13:1-17).

This particular passage tells us what Jesus *did,* what Jesus *is now doing* and what Jesus *wants us to do.*

What Jesus Did

What did Jesus do? *He humbled Himself.* John 13 is an illustration of Philippians 2:5-8. Our Lord Jesus

Christ, though He was God, did not count equality with God as something to be held onto selfishly, but He emptied Himself and made Himself of no reputation. He humbled Himself and became obedient even to death on the cross. John 13 is an illustration of what happened when our Lord Jesus came to this earth, was born as a baby, grew up and became God's suffering servant.

What Jesus Does Now

John 13 also tells us what Jesus is now doing. What is He doing? *Keeping His own people clean.* There is an important distinction in verse 10 between being washed all over—bathed—and simply having your feet washed. Today we don't worry much about the problem of soiled feet, but back in New Testament days they had to worry about it. Many people did not wear shoes, and those who did wore simple sandals. The streets were not paved, and people got their feet dirty. When guests came to your home, they would leave their sandals at the door, and then someone—the host or a servant—would wash the guests' feet. This was an important part of hospitality.

When you were saved, you were washed all over. But as you walk through this world, your feet get dirty. It is important for you to come to the Lord and to let Him cleanse you. This is not the once-and-for-all washing of salvation; it is that daily, moment-by-moment cleansing of sanctification. John 13 is an illustration of I John 1:9: "If we confess our sins, he is faithful and just to forgive us our sins, and to cleanse us from all unrighteousness."

So if you have been saved and then you have gotten into some kind of sin, you do not need to be saved all over again. You have been washed, but you do need to have your feet cleansed. This is done by confessing that sin to the Lord Jesus Christ.

What Jesus Wants Us to Do

We have discovered what Jesus did and what Jesus is doing. But the important lesson in John 13 is what Jesus wants us to do. What does He want us to do? *Follow His example.* "I have given you an example, that ye should do as I have done to you" (v. 15). He did not say that we should do *what* He did—that would mean taking all of this very literally. We are to do *as* He did. He gave us an example of humility, of putting Himself at the feet of others to serve them.

Example of Humility

What does it mean to wash one another's feet? It means to humble ourselves before one another, to minister to one another, to take the place of a servant. Occasionally the host, as an honor, would wash the guests' feet, but usually this was done by servants. Our Lord was the host at the Last Supper. But He is also God! Can you imagine God's bowing before sinful men and washing their feet? "I have given you an example," said Jesus (John 13:15)—an

15

example of humility, an example of service, an example of putting others on a higher level than yourself.

This touches us where it really hurts! We live in a world that asks, "How high are you? What is your position?" Our Lord asks, "How low are you? Are you washing others' feet?"

The disciples, as you know, often argued over who was, or would be, the greatest. On a couple of occasions in the four Gospels our Lord Jesus rebuked them. We have this problem today. When you read some magazines and some press releases, you find people fighting over who is the greatest—who has the greatest church, who is the greatest preacher. Our Lord says the important thing is to be the greatest servant.

"The servant is not greater than his lord" (v. 16). If my Lord humbled Himself and washed the disciples' feet, who am I that I should not do this? "Neither he that is sent greater than he that sent him. If ye know these things, happy are ye if ye do them" (vv. 16,17). Something in my nature does not want to get down before anybody else and be a servant. And yet Jesus tells us that the happiest life is the life of service.

Secret of Humility

I have noted in my Bible that John 13:3 says, "Jesus knowing that the Father had given all things into his hands." Verse 4 reads: "He . . . took a towel." If you had *everything* in your hands, would

16

you take a towel? I certainly would not! If I had everything in my hands, given to me from God, I would be using it for my own enjoyment. Jesus Christ said, "I have everything in My hands. My Father has given Me everything. I am going to set that aside now and take up a towel. I am going to become a servant." This is the secret of humility.

Humility comes when we realize God has given us everything. We don't have to pretend. We don't have to act as though we are important. We don't have to tell people how big we are—*we have everything.* "All things are your's" (I Cor. 3:21). Everything has been put into our hands through Jesus Christ. We don't have to fight for anything, we don't have to struggle for anything—it is all ours. We possess all things through Jesus Christ (see vv. 22,23).

When you realize this great truth, you can reach out, take up a towel and serve other people. If Jesus Christ, the very Son of God, could do this, we should do it as well. He did it for *us,* and we should do it for *others.*

Practice of Humility

What does it mean to wash others' feet? It means to be a blessing to them. It means to help them keep clean. It means to refresh them. The Apostle Paul often wrote in his epistles about people who had refreshed him. In I Corinthians 16:17,18 he wrote about some of the saints who had come and refreshed him. He talked about these people in glowing terms because they had refreshed him in the things of the Lord. He repeated this idea in Romans 15:30-33, in II Corinthians 7:24, in II Timothy 1:16-18 and in the little Book of Philemon (1:7,20).

Do you refresh anybody? When you are with people, does the life of God flow through you so that you refresh people? Or do you dry people out? Do you bore people spiritually?

Have you ever traced the word "water" in the Gospel of John? In John 4:13,14, Jesus told the woman at the well that He would put *within* her a well of living water. We ask the obvious question: Where does that water flow? John 7:37-39 answers the question. The Lord Jesus cried, "If any man thirst, let him come unto me, and drink. . . . Out of his belly [innermost being] shall flow rivers of living water" (vv. 37,38). The well of living water that refreshed *me* on the inside becomes a river of living water to flow out and touch *your* life and refresh *you.*

Some people have a hard time serving other people. They can't open a car door for someone else. They can't do anything for anybody else. Other people seem to exist just to serve others. Our Lord said that if you want to experience holiness and if you want to experience happiness, practice humility. That is the summary of this whole chapter. Where there is humility of heart, there is holiness of life. And when you combine humility and holiness, you have happiness. "If ye know these things, happy are ye if ye do them" (13:17).

18

So the next time we have the opportunity, let's serve others. The next time we have the opportunity, let's refresh others. Let's wash their feet. You say, "Well, that means being a servant." That's right. But when you are a servant in the will of God, it is such a thrilling, wonderful thing! I know it is not easy to be a servant. We have to pray and ask the Holy Spirit to help us. We are so prone to defend ourselves and to want everybody else to serve us. But how wonderful it is when we experience the humility and the happiness and the holiness of a life that is yielded to Christ, a life of serving others, of washing one another's feet.

Receive One Another

Christians who care will receive one another.

"Him that is weak in the faith receive ye, but not to doubtful disputations" (Rom. 14:1). That second phrase may be translated, "Not for disputes about doubtful things." In Romans 15:7 we read: "Wherefore receive ye one another, as Christ also received us to the glory of God."

In Romans 14 and 15 Paul was dealing with the problem of division in the church. In this particular fellowship, the believers were divided over diets and days. The weak Christians would eat only vegetables; the strong Christians realized that they could eat anything because all food had been declared clean by the Lord Jesus Christ. The weak Christians would commemorate special holy days, whereas the strong Christians esteemed all days as special to the Lord. Sad to say, the weak Christians were judging the strong Christians, and the strong Christians were despising the weak Christians.

Paul identified himself with the strong Christians. "We then that are strong ought to bear the infirmities of the weak, and not to please ourselves" (15:1). In these two chapters Paul gave three admonitions for us to obey if we are going to have harmony in the church: *Receive one another* (14:1-12), *edify one another* (14:13-23) and *please one another* (15:1-7).

Christians do not always agree. They do not agree about religious celebrations or about certain religious practices. You could divide a church a dozen ways if you started arguing about areas of disagreement! I have known people to disagree over Bible translations or over whether or not to participate in certain ministries or amusements. Paul laid down a very practical admonition: "Receive one another, and don't argue. Receive one another, but not for the purpose of carrying on disputes." He was writing, of course, about receiving people into the local fellowship. He was discussing Christians who are disagreeable about their disagreements.

The weak Christian, of course, is the one who is all wrapped up in rules and regulations. The weak Christians in the fellowship probably had been saved out of Judaism, and they were still devoted to the Law of the Old Testament. The strong Christians (who could have been either Jews or Gentiles) realized that in Jesus Christ there is freedom from the Old Testament Law. The righteousness of the Law is still God's standard. According to Romans 8:1-4, the righteousness of the Law is being fulfilled in us by the Holy Spirit as we walk in the Spirit. But we are not obligated to obey all of those detailed laws that were given through Moses. The strong Christians enjoyed their liberty and despised the legalistic, weak Christians. The weak Christians continued in their immaturity and condemned the strong Christians!

This situation reminds me of a family with a big

brother and a little brother. The big brother has privileges the little brother does not have. If the little brother dared to do some of the things that the big brother is able to do, it would hurt him. But the big brother looks down at the little brother and says, "You're just a little kid—you can't do the things I do!"

Sometimes we see this attitude in churches where strong Christians are careless and even defiant in their relationship to the weaker and younger Christians. This leads to disputing (14:1), despising (v. 3) and even denouncing, or judging, (v. 3). It is not a happy situation.

Paul gave four very practical reasons why we should receive one another and not argue with one another about these minor differences. Please keep in mind that we are not talking about major doctrines. We are not talking about the Incarnation of Jesus Christ, the resurrection or the inspiration of the Bible. These are cardinal, fundamental doctrines about which all Christians agree. We are talking about minor matters about which Christians sometimes disagree.

God Has Received Us

The first reason we should receive one another is *because God has received us.* "Him that is weak in the faith receive ye, but not to doubtful disputations. For one believeth that he may eat all things: another, who is weak, eateth herbs. Let not him that eateth despise him that eateth not; and let not

22

him which eateth not judge him that eateth: for God hath received him" (Rom. 14:1-3).

If God the Father has received me into His family, what right do you have to reject me? If the Father has received you into the family, what right have I to reject you? The Father has received us; God has opened the door.

God spoke to Peter and said, "Peter, I want you to go to the Gentiles" (see Acts 10). Peter said, "Not so, Lord! They are unclean!" (see v. 14). God said, "Don't you call anybody unclean that I have declared clean" (see v. 15). So Peter went to the Gentiles and preached the gospel. The group he preached to accepted Christ as their Saviour, and a wonderful blessing came to the household of Cornelius. The church in Jerusalem heard about this new movement and called Peter on the carpet (see Acts 11). Peter's reply was simple: "The Holy Spirit came upon them just as He did upon us, and they trusted Christ. Therefore, since God has accepted them, I have to accept them" (see vv. 15-17). The Jewish Christians then said, "Isn't this marvelous? God has given the gift of repentance to the Gentiles" (see v. 18). Paul went out to minister to the Gentiles, and he came home and reported that God had opened the door of faith to the Gentiles. But some of the legalistic Jewish believers wanted to close the door! When God has received someone, you have to receive him. You may have disagreements with him, but you have to receive him. The first reason for receiving one another is that God has received us.

God Sustains Us

The second reason is in Romans 14:4: *God sustains us.* "Who art thou that judgest another man's servant? to his own master he standeth or falleth. Yea, he shall be holden up: for God is able to make him stand." God not only receives us, but God also enables us to stand.

We do need each other. There is no such thing in the New Testament as an isolated Christian outside the church fellowship. Many try to live that way today, but that is not New Testament Christianity. According to the New Testament, when you trust Jesus as your Saviour, you become a part of a local fellowship, you go to work for God, and you try to help each other.

But verse 4 warns us that God is the One who enables His servant to stand. Since God is able to sustain him, we ought to receive him. We sometimes look at people and say, "Well, we can do without them; we don't need them in our fellowship." That is a dangerous thing to say. The person that we will not receive, who has the right to be received, may be just the one we really need. God sustains him; therefore, we should receive him.

Jesus Christ Is Lord

In Romans 14:5-9 Paul gave the third reason why we ought to receive one another. Not only does God receive us and sustain us, but also *Jesus Christ is Lord.* "One man esteemeth one day above

24

another: another esteemeth every day alike. Let every man be fully persuaded in his own mind. He that regardeth the day, regardeth it unto the Lord; and he that regardeth not the day, to the Lord he doth not regard it. He that eateth [meat], eateth to the Lord, for he giveth God thanks; and he that eateth not, to the Lord he eateth not, and giveth God thanks" (vv. 5,6).

The emphasis is on the lordship of Jesus Christ. "For none of us liveth to himself, and no man dieth to himself. For whether we live, we live unto the Lord; and whether we die, we die unto the Lord: whether we live therefore, or die, we are the Lord's. For to this end Christ both died, and rose, and revived, that he might be Lord both of the dead and living" (vv. 7-9). Eight times in this passage Paul mentioned "the Lord." Jesus is Lord. I am not lord over you, and you must not be lord over me. Jesus Christ is the Lord. He is the Lord by nature because He is God, and He is the Lord by right because He died for us and rose again that He might be Lord.

I fear we have too many "junior gods" running around today, taking the place of God in the lives of others. Some weak Christians seemingly cannot do a thing unless they check with somebody. It is good to have guidance from mature believers, but God says that Jesus is Lord. Please don't let any person take the place of God in your life.

In John 21, the Lord Jesus said to Peter, "Follow me" (v. 19). So Peter began to follow the Lord. Then Peter heard footsteps behind him, so he turned around. That was a dangerous thing to do—he got

25

his eyes off the Lord, and he saw John. Peter said to Jesus, "Lord, and what shall this man do?" (v. 21). Jesus answered, "What is that to thee? follow thou me" (v. 22).

I do not have the right to tell you what God wants to do in your life. I can pray with you, I can counsel you, I can show you the Word; but I cannot take the place of God in your life. Weak, immature Christians are always looking for crutches and props and substitutes. Mature Christians realize that Jesus is Lord, and because Jesus is Lord, we cannot judge one another. Because Jesus is Lord, we cannot criticize one another or argue with one another about trifles. He is Lord.

Jesus Christ Is the Judge

Finally, in Romans 14:10-12 we see the fourth reason why we should receive one another: *Jesus Christ is the Judge.* He is not only Lord, but He is also the Judge. "But why dost thou judge thy brother? or why dost thou set at nought thy brother? for we shall all stand before the judgment seat of Christ" (v. 10). You are not going to be sitting on that judgment seat; I'm not going to be sitting there. We are going to be standing there. Our Lord Jesus is the Judge. "For it is written, As I live, saith the Lord, every knee shall bow to me, and every tongue shall confess to God. So then every one of us shall give account of himself to God" (vv. 11,12).

The Lord is not going to ask you to give an

accounting for me; He is not going to ask me to give an accounting for you. You must give your own account; I must give my account, and there is no escape. If we would spend less time criticizing one another and judging one another and spend more time judging ourselves and evaluating our own lives, we would be in better shape to stand before the Judgment Seat of Christ.

Please remember these four reasons why we should receive one another and not argue about minor things. *God has received us*—we have no right to reject anyone whom God has received. *God sustains us. Jesus Christ is Lord. Jesus Christ is the Judge.* The next time you are tempted to reject some believer, just remember that he belongs to God's family because God has received him. If he is truly a believer, God will sustain him. God may do through him something that you really need to have done to you. Jesus Christ is Lord, and we have no right to reject anybody until our Lord tells us to. Jesus Christ is the Judge. I think a lot of things are going to be straightened out at the Judgment Seat of Christ, particularly divisions, dissensions and disputes over minor matters that kept us from obeying His commandment: "Wherefore receive ye one another, as Christ also received us to the glory of God" (15:7).

Chapter 4

Edify One Another

Christians who care edify one another.

The word "edify" means "to build up." It comes from a Latin word which means "to build." Our English word "edifice" comes from that same word. Christians who care edify one another—they build one another up in the faith. "Let us therefore follow after the things which make for peace, and things wherewith one may edify another" (Rom. 14:19).

How can I help you grow as a Christian? How can you help me to grow? Each of us is a part of a local fellowship—at least we ought to be. And in that local fellowship we must minister to one another. One way we minister to one another is by edifying one another.

There are two kinds of people in this world—those who destroy and those who build. There are those who edify, and there are those who tear down. It takes very little effort and very little intelligence to tear down, but it takes something out of you to build up another person. It is much easier to be a destroyer than to be a builder, but God wants us to be builders. He does not want us to go through life tearing down other people, churches and Sunday school classes. He wants us to edify one another.

Our Example

God has given us several spiritual tools that we can use for building up one another. The first tool for edifying one another is *our example* (Rom. 14:14-21).

In Romans 14 Paul was discussing the problem of disagreement among Christians. You will recall that the weak Christians would eat only vegetables, and they were judging the strong Christians who believed, rightly so, that they could eat all things. And so there was division in the church—arguments over trifles and nonessentials—and this brought about dissension and division.

Paul said, "Receive ye" (v. 1). And then he said, "Edify one another" (see v. 19). "Let us not therefore judge one another any more," he wrote in verse 13, "but judge this rather, that no man put a stumblingblock or an occasion to fall in his brother's way." We affect each other. "I know, and am persuaded by the Lord Jesus, that there is nothing unclean of itself: but to him that esteemeth any thing to be unclean, to him it is unclean. But if thy brother be grieved with thy meat, now walkest thou not charitably [in love]. Destroy not him with thy meat, for whom Christ died. Let not then your good be evil spoken of: for the kingdom of God is not meat and drink; but righteousness, and peace, and joy in the Holy Ghost [Spirit]" (vv. 14-17). In other words, the example of the strong Christian should encourage the weak Christian to grow.

We must be very careful not to run ahead of

someone's Christian experience. We must not force our maturity on someone else. You cannot force a baby to grow. In fact, there are stages in a child's life when it takes a great deal of patience, love and kindness to bring the child to maturity.

In Jesus Christ we have freedom, but if we use that freedom selfishly, we'll destroy somebody else. I can go places that might not hurt me, but they might hurt somebody else. I could engage in certain activities as a growing Christian that would not destroy me, but they might destroy someone else. When my wife and I were first married, we were not too careful about whether or not we left knives on the table or scissors on the floor. But when the children came along, we checked to make sure that the knives were put away and that there were no scissors or pins on the floor. Would it have been a sin for my wife to leave a pin on the floor? No, but if that pin hurt somebody else—a little child on the floor—then she would have done harm.

So the first tool we have for edifying one another is our own example. Is your example as a Christian tearing people down or building them up?

Our Speech

The second tool that we have is *our speech*. "Let no corrupt communication proceed out of your mouth, but that which is good to the use of edifying, that it may minister grace unto the hearers" (Eph. 4:29). As we speak to one another, we are either building up or tearing down.

30

You cannot see spoken words. We can attach electronic devices to a microphone, and then we could see the impact of the words electrically, but we cannot see the spoken words. Words have power: words are able to build up or to tear down. Have you ever had the experience of someone's coming to you on a dark, dismal day and just speaking a word of encouragement? Their words make the sun come out! On the other hand, have you ever had the experience, when you are feeling fine, of someone's coming along and criticizing you? Or perhaps you received a letter that was critical. And then the sun disappeared. Words have power.

We are told in Ephesians 4:15, "But speaking the truth in love, may grow up into him." We need both truth and love. As we speak the truth in love, we are able to build people up. It has well been said that love without truth is hypocrisy, and truth without love is brutality. We do not want either one. We want to speak the truth in love. Our words should minister grace to the hearers. Our speech ought to always be "with grace, seasoned with salt," we are told in Colossians 4:6. There ought always to be a graciousness about our speech that comes from a heart filled with love. We edify one another by our example, and we edify one another by our speech.

Our Spiritual Gifts

God gives us a third tool for the edifying of the church—*the ministry of our spiritual gifts.* "Even so ye, forasmuch as ye are zealous of spiritual gifts,

31

seek that ye may excel to the edifying of the church" (I Cor. 14:12). "Let all things be done unto edifying" (v. 26).

As you know, the Corinthian church was all wrapped up in spiritual gifts. They were competing with one another. They were a very gifted church; in fact, Paul stated that they did not lack any gift (1:4-7). But they were using those gifts as toys to play with and as weapons to fight with, not as tools to build with. They were competing with one another. They were "showing off" with their spiritual gifts. God gave us spiritual gifts, not to show off, not to build up our own egos but to build up one another.

In fact, the services held by the Corinthian assembly were not building up at all; they were tearing down. Paul said, "When you meet together it is not for the better but for the worse" (11:17, Amplified). It is unfortunate that when some of God's people get together, there is rivalry, bickering and competition instead of unity. People go home, not having been built up but having been torn down. "Let all things be done unto edifying" (14:26).

This means that when the church gathers together, the hymns ought to be edifying, the teaching and the preaching ought to be edifying. Even the fellowshipping over food ought to be edifying as the church gathers together to eat. There certainly is nothing wrong with eating, but the fellowship ought to be edifying. We ought to use our spiritual gifts to build up other Christians.

I think too often we go to church with this attitude: "Well, what am I going to get out of it?" Then we come home and say, "I didn't get anything out of it!" But we ought to go to the assembly saying, "What can I put into it? How can I help somebody else grow in the Lord?" That word of encouragement, that brief time of fellowship could mean so much in the life of some other Christian. So the next time you find yourself with God's people in God's house, say to yourself, "I want to help others grow today."

Our Love

God gives us a fourth tool for building up one another. First Corinthians 8:1 states, "Knowledge puffeth up, but charity [love] edifieth." *Love edifies.*

All of us know people who are smart, but all they do is tear things down. They have a great knowledge of the Word of God, but they tear down; they do not build up. Their knowledge of the Word of God has become a weapon they use as they go from church to church. Paul said, in effect, "You have knowledge, and that is fine. But knowledge will puff up and inflate your ego. Love will build up." He was not saying that we have to make a choice between love and knowledge, because God wants us to speak "the truth in love" (Eph. 4:15). He was saying that we should use our knowledge in love. When you sing your song, do it in love. Whatever you are doing for God, do it in love. Love always builds up.

This means I must have the love of God in my heart. This all relates to what Jesus said to His disciples: "A new commandment I give unto you,

33

That ye love one another" (John 13:34). It is impossible to build people up in hatred, in criticism or in strife. Love builds up.

This love shows itself in so many ways. First Corinthians 13 describes it. Love shows itself in patience, in kindness and in gentleness. Love builds up, and love is the foundation for everything that we do.

Our Prayer

We build each other up by our example, by our speech, by our ministry of spiritual gifts and by love. Colossians 4:12 tells us that we build each other up through *prayer*. This verse is about Epaphras, one of the Apostle Paul's associates: "A servant of Christ, saluteth you, always labouring fervently for you in prayers, that ye may stand perfect and complete in all the will of God." As we pray for people, then God is able to work and to build them up. We build up one another through prayer.

I hope you have a prayer list. I hope you don't just pray generally, "Lord, bless the church and bless our Sunday school class." Pray *specifically*. I suggest you take the names of the people about whom you are concerned, divide them by seven, and pray for a certain number each day. It is a wonderful thing to pray specifically for people because God uses prayer to build people up in the faith.

God's Word

In Acts 20:32 Paul said, "And now, brethren, I

commend you to God, and to the word of his grace, which is able to build you up." The Word of God is a great tool for building up one another. When you are discussing problems with people, use the Word of God. When folks call to complain about something, use the Word of God. Drop the Word of God into your conversation. Share the Word of God. Don't go around beating people over the head with the Bible. Don't go around quoting Scripture all the time. But do use the Word of God discreetly because it builds people up.

As we close this study, let me ask you a question: Are you a destroyer, or are you a builder? Is God using you to build up the church, to build up other saints? I trust that He is using us to build others, because Christians who care edify one another.

Chapter 5

Do Not Judge One Another

Christians who care do not judge one another.

"Let us not therefore judge one another any more" (Rom. 14:13). "Let not him that eateth despise him that eateth not; and let not him which eateth not judge him that eateth: for God hath received him" (v. 3). Let us not judge one another.

A great deal of judging goes on, doesn't it? I wonder sometimes if judging one another is not the chief "indoor sport" of some of God's people. Paul laid down some important guidelines for us in Romans and in some other epistles to help us in this matter of judging.

We Must Have Discernment

To begin with, *we must have discernment in the Christian life.* Christian love is not blind. Paul prayed for the Philippians: "And this I pray, that your love may abound yet more and more in knowledge and in all judgment [discernment]; that ye may approve things that are excellent; that ye may be sincere and without offence till the day of Christ" (Phil. 1:9,10). His prayer was that they might have discernment—loving discernment, careful discernment. Christians have to exercise discernment. We don't walk around with our eyes closed.

I know some people tell us that love is so great and so wonderful that we should just love everybody regardless. We are to love one another, and we are to love lost souls. Certainly we are to love our enemies. But in exercising this love we must have discernment. Christian love is not blind. In the Sermon on the Mount our Lord Jesus said, "Do not cast your pearls before swine. Do not give that which is holy to the dogs" (see Matt. 7:6). I am going to have to exercise discernment to know who are the swine and who are the dogs and who are the sheep! We do not distribute the treasures of the grace of God indiscriminantly. We must exercise discernment. However, discernment, if we are not careful, can turn into a judgmental attitude. In trying to be true to God, we may get so critical, so judgmental, so condemning that nothing is right except what we do. Nothing is good except what we like. We do have to exercise discernment. That's the first principle we must learn.

We Must Start With Ourselves

The second guideline is simply this: *We have to start with ourselves.* In the Bible we are not told that it is wrong to help a brother by pointing out his weaknesses. What we are told is that we must start by examining ourselves (Matt. 7). "Judge not, that ye be not judged" (v. 1). If we stopped right there, people would say, "See, it is *always* wrong to judge." But read the rest of the passage. "For with what judgment ye judge, ye shall be judged: and

37

with what measure ye mete, it shall be measured to you again" (v. 2). In other words, you get back just what you give. If you are going to be critical of other people, they are going to be critical of you.

Let me say a word to my fellow pastors. When you stand in that pulpit, your people become what you are. If you are judgmental and critical, they will be judgmental and critical. We must be very careful.

"And why beholdest thou the mote [the little speck] that is in thy brother's eye, but considerest not the beam that is in thine own eye? Or how wilt thou say to thy brother, Let me pull out the mote out of thine eye; and, behold, a beam is in thine own eye?" (vv. 3,4). The crowd must have laughed out loud when Jesus said this. Eastern people love exaggeration and contrast. They could visualize a doctor trying to take a speck out of a patient's eye while having a two-by-four in his own eye!

I once was playing soccer on the school field when I was in junior high school, and construction was going on nearby. A piece of cement lodged in my eye. They had to take me to an eye doctor. I will never forget how this lady bent over me, put a special magnifying device over her eye and picked out that little piece of cement from my eye. It felt so good to get rid of it! But suppose there had been something in her own eye so that she could not see!

Our Lord was laying down a principle in Matthew 7. He said, in effect, "By all means try to help your brother, but start with yourself."

"Thou hypocrite, first cast out the beam out of thine own eye; and then shalt thou see clearly to cast out the mote out of thy brother's eye" (v. 5). So we do have to have discernment, and we do have the responsibility of helping our brother, but we must begin with ourselves.

I have not always followed this principle, and I have suffered for it. I'm praying that God will help me to follow it. Before we criticize our brother, we should see if perhaps there is something worse in our own life. I'll tell you what this does for you: It helps you to see your brother a lot more clearly. It also gives you a great deal more compassion. I don't want an eye doctor operating on my eye with a crowbar and a pipe wrench! I want tenderness and delicacy and compassion because the eye is one of the most sensitive parts of the human body. So we don't rush up to people to condemn and judge. We first examine our own lives to see if there is something that we need to deal with. We do need discernment, but we must begin with ourselves.

Jesus Christ Is Lord

In Romans 14 Paul gave several other guidelines, and these are very important. He said, for example, that *Jesus Christ is Lord.* Jesus Christ may want to use us to help a brother, but He is Lord. We are not to play God in the lives of others. "For to this end Christ both died, and rose, and revived, that he might be Lord both of the dead and living. But why dost thou judge thy brother?" (vv. 9,10). He was talking about the weak Christians who were judging the strong Christians. "Why dost thou set at nought

39

thy brother?" (v. 10). That's a reference to the strong Christians. They were despising the weak Christians. "For we shall all stand before the judgment seat of Christ" (v. 10).

I have no right to judge my brother as though I were the Lord Jesus. All of us have been judged by others in one way or another. Those of us who minister widely, by means of radio and in other ways, sometimes get very critical letters from people. We wonder sometimes if they have really prayed and thought the matter through. But we must remember that Jesus is Lord. I must never take the place of Jesus in somebody's life. I cannot do it. If I am going to pass judgment on you, I must first come to the Lord and let Him be the Lord of my life. I must say, "O Lord Jesus, You are God, You are the Judge. Now, if You want me to deal with my brother, show me from the Word and give me guidance by the Holy Spirit because I cannot do this myself." If I do it myself, certainly I am going to fail and cause trouble.

We Must Have Priorities

Paul made another statement and laid down another guideline. He instructed us *to have priorities and to deal with the things that are important.* "I know, and am persuaded by the Lord Jesus, that there is nothing unclean of itself" (Rom. 14:14). Under the old economy in the Old Testament, there were clean and unclean foods. All of this was a part of God's training of His people in preparation for the

40

time when Jesus would come and redeem His people. But when our Lord died and rose again, when the Holy Spirit came, all of these distinctions were erased—and today there is no such thing as clean or unclean food. Some food may not be good for you, but that's another matter. Concerning the spiritual consequences of what you eat, the Word of God makes it very clear that one kind of food is just like another.

The weak Christians in the church were going by rules and regulations. They were quite legalistic. They said, "Christians cannot eat everything!" The strong Christians, who really had faith and believed the Word of God, said, "Yes, we can eat everything." And so there was a division. "To him that esteemeth any thing to be unclean, to him it is unclean. But if thy brother be grieved with thy meat [food], now walkest thou not charitably [in love]. Destroy not him with thy meat [food], for whom Christ died" (vv. 14,15). Paul was reminding us to have priorities.

"For meat [food] destroy not the work of God" (v. 20). Perhaps you heard about the farmer who was out working in his field. He saw a mouse, and that angered him. So he took his hoe and began to go after that mouse. He spent the next 30 minutes chasing and beating at that mouse, and he finally killed him. Then he looked and realized he had wrecked an acre of his crops. Was it worth it? Probably not.

You see, we must have priorities. Some things are more important than other things, and to destroy a fellow Christian over the matter of eating and drinking is simply not worth it. To destroy a Sunday school class over which Bible translation to use is simply not worth it. To destroy a church over what kind of music to allow is simply not worth it. We must have priorities. Paul said in Romans 14:21, "It is good neither to eat flesh [meat], nor to drink wine, nor [to do] any thing whereby thy brother stumbleth, or is offended, or is made weak." Your Christian brother is important, even though he may be a weak brother, even though he may be slow in growing in the Lord. But we must not destroy the work of God for the sake of our own prejudices and opinions. We must have priorities.

We Must Show Love and Patience

Finally, *we must show love and patience*. "We then that are strong ought to bear the infirmities of the weak, and not to please ourselves. Let every one of us please his neighbour for his good to edification" (Rom. 15:1,2). Notice that it says "for his good." We don't always please our children, because some of the things they want are not for their good. But as much as possible, the strong Christians (who are walking in the freedom of God) ought to please the weak Christians so they can lovingly help them grow.

Parents do this. They adjust their schedule to that of the baby. We adjust our plans to the schooling of the children. We have to adjust our living to the weaknesses of our children. This is the only way

42

they will ever grow up. So the strong Christians in the fellowship have to consider the weak Christians and not selfishly please themselves.

We need discernment, and we must start with ourselves when it comes to judging. We must have priorities—don't destroy God's work for something unimportant. We must show love and patience, and as much as possible, we must try to please the weaker Christians for their good.

It is not wrong to exercise judgment; it is wrong to be judgmental. It is not wrong to have discernment—how we need discernment these days! But it is wrong to think we are the only ones who are right. We must remember that Jesus Christ is Lord. The lordship of Jesus Christ solves so many problems. I think it is important that you and I (and I speak to my own heart here) forsake a judgmental attitude. We must help our Christian brother; we must be tender and loving, patient and kind. We must seek as much as possible to help our brother grow.

Christians who care do not judge one another.

Chapter 6

Bear One Another's Burdens

Caring Christians bear one another's burdens.

"Brethren, if a man be overtaken in a fault, ye which are spiritual, restore such an one in the spirit of meekness; considering thyself, lest thou also be tempted. Bear ye one another's burdens, and so fulfil the law of Christ. For if a man think himself to be something, when he is nothing, he deceiveth himself. But let every man prove his own work, and then shall he have rejoicing in himself alone, and not in another. For every man shall bear his own burden" (Gal. 6:1-5).

There seems to be a contradiction between Galatians 6:2 and Galatians 6:5, but there is not. In Galatians 6:2 the word for "burdens" refers to a heavy load, a trial, something that is very difficult to bear. In verse 5 the word refers to a little load you carry on your back. This word was used for a soldier's pack.

I have certain burdens that only I can bear. I can't pass my responsibilities to others because I have to fulfill that work myself. I have to be the husband and the father in my home; I have to do the work that God has called me to do. Therefore, I have to bear my own burden. Every soldier has to shoulder his own pack. Those people who try to give their responsibilities to somebody else are missing a blessing and are disobeying God. So verse 5 is talking about the responsibilities of ministry, but verse 2 is talking about the burdens of life that are so heavy to carry, the trials that come to us as believers. The admonition is "Bear ye one another's burdens, and so fulfil the law of Christ."

This admonition is in the context of restoring a brother who has sinned. If someone in the church has been overtaken by a fault—he was tempted and he failed—our responsibility is to help him bear that burden.

There are many burdens that we can help people carry. That is one of the beautiful things about the fellowship of the church. As we fellowship together in the things of the Lord, we can help one another. We can help one another materially and physically. We can help each other financially. There are many ways that we as Christians can help to bear burdens. The particular way that is emphasized in Galatians 6 is helping those who have stumbled and fallen.

Paul gave us three instructions in this paragraph. He explained *what we should do*—restore. He told us *why we should do it*—because of the law of Christ, which is the law of love. Then he stated *how we should do it*—with meekness. "Bear ye one another's burdens, and so fulfil the law of Christ" (v. 2).

45

What We Should Do

Our responsibility is found in the word "restore": "Brethren, if a man be overtaken in a fault, ye which are spiritual, restore such an one in the spirit of meekness" (Gal. 6:1).

No Rejoicing

This word "restore" is not the word "rejoice." It does not say you should rejoice if someone sins. Some people enjoy it when other Christians fall—they think it makes *them* look good. I would remind you that when one member of the body hurts, it hurts all of us. The eye cannot say, "I'm glad I don't have a tack in me—the tack is in the foot." Well, that tack in the foot might fester and get infected, and it could one day affect the eye! There is no such thing as one believer's fall being used to help another believer. Galatians 6:1 does not say to rejoice.

No Revealing

It does not say "reveal." We are not to expose the sin of a fellow believer. Some Christians love to do this. When Noah got drunk, he was lying in his tent naked, and Ham laughed at him and made sport of him (see Gen. 9:20-23). Noah's other sons backed into the tent and covered their father. Love covers a multitude of sins—it doesn't go around revealing them.

46

Love does not cleanse sin—grace does that. Love does not condone sin, but love does cover sin. There is no reason to hang dirty wash out in public. The Bible does not say "rejoice," it does not say "reveal," it does not say "reject." It does not say, "If somebody falls into sin, reject him, judge him, condemn him." The Pharisees did this, and this was wrong. The Bible says "restore."

The doctors knew this word because it was a medical term used in referring to setting a broken bone. The Church is Christ's Body, and if a member of the Church is out of the will of God and falls into sin, it is like having a broken bone. That bone has to be set. The only way to set a broken bone is with tenderness. If it isn't set properly, it is going to create problems. I have a friend who recently had to have his arm broken and reset because it hadn't been done properly a few years ago. The doctors knew this word—it meant to set a broken bone.

The fishermen knew this word because it meant "to mend the nets." It is translated that way in Matthew 4:21—"mending their nets." If nets are not mended, you can't use them. If Christians are not restored, God cannot use them to catch "fish" or to serve others.

The soldiers knew this word—it meant "to equip an army." Unless we help to restore those who have sinned, they will never be able to win the battles of life. We aren't just restoring a brother or a sister, we

47

are helping to equip a soldier to go out and fight the battle.

The sailors knew this word. It meant "to outfit a ship for a voyage." Each of us has to face the storms of life. Each of us has to carry some cargo to the glory of God. But if the Christian is not restored, he cannot do it.

So this word refers to setting a broken bone, to mending nets, to equipping an army and to outfitting a ship. That is what we are doing when we help another Christian. We bear one another's burdens when we help to restore a believer who has failed.

Do you know somebody who has sinned? Is there somebody in your church fellowship, your Sunday school class, your family who has gotten out of the will of God? What is your attitude toward that person? Are you rejoicing? Are you revealing their sin all over the place? Are you rejecting that person? God's Word says you should help to *restore* that person.

Why We Should Do It

In the second instruction, Paul told us *why we should do it.* "Bear ye one another's burdens, and so fulfil the law of Christ" (Gal. 6:2). We know what the law of Christ is: "A new commandment I give unto you, That ye love one another" (John 13:34). This command is repeated several times in the New Testament as we have discovered in Chapter 1. "Love one another"—that's the law of Christ. We don't restore people because of law; we do it because of love. Legalists don't know much about restoring people. A legalist has nothing to restore anybody with. The Pharisees were quick to judge and to condemn, but they had no love in their hearts. If someone did not meet their standards, they had nothing to do with that person.

Paul addressed his readers as brothers (Gal. 6:1). Restoring another Christian is a *family matter*. We love the members of the family. We care for the household of faith. "As we have therefore opportunity, let us do good unto all men, especially unto them who are of the household of faith" (v. 10). When you have love for other believers, you will help to restore those who have sinned.

It is marvelous to operate by love and not by law! The law of love takes care of all other laws. Love is the fulfillment of the Law. We can help a brother— we can carry his burdens, we can help him to be restored—if we love him.

You may disagree with this, but I believe this with my whole heart: The way we treat a brother who has sinned is evidence of our own spiritual condition. Legalists always condemn, but those who love Jesus Christ and are mature always try to restore. What should we do? Restore. Why should we do it? Because of love, not law.

How We Should Do It

"Restore such an one in the spirit of meekness" (Gal. 6:1). Meekness is not weakness. Meekness is power under control. The meek person is filled with

49

the Holy Spirit, because part of the fruit of the Spirit is meekness (5:22,23). Our Lord, in the Beatitudes, said, "Blessed are the meek: for they shall inherit the earth" (Matt. 5:5). God can use those who have power under control.

Let's go back to the illustrations mentioned in our first point. Doctors, when they set a broken bone, have power under control. They don't use a crowbar or a pipe wrench! They are gentle—they use power under control. Would you call a doctor weak because he showed power under control? No, we would say he was very strong.

How are you going to equip an army with weakness? How are you going to outfit a ship with weakness? How do you mend a net with weakness? Each of these illustrations pictures power under control, not weakness. We should have a spirit of meekness because, in restoring people, we might hurt them all the more. How careful we have to be!

But the main point Paul made was this: "Considering thyself, lest thou also be tempted" (Gal. 6:1). What we think of ourselves determines how we treat other people. I want to repeat that—it may be a whole new idea to you. *What you think of yourself will determine how you treat other people.* Our Lord said this in the so-called Golden Rule: "Whatsoever ye would that men should do to you, do ye even so to them" (Matt. 7:12). If you say, *"I could have sinned. It could have been me who was falling, or stumbling,"* then you will treat a person with meekness and with gentleness. But if you say, "Well, that could never happen to *me. I* would never do a thing like that!" then you are going to have trouble.

The hidden cause of refusing to help people is pride. "If a man think himself to be something, when he is nothing, he deceiveth himself" (Gal. 6:3). "I don't need any help," says the proud person. "I would never do a thing like that!" Paul warned us that we had better have meekness because we may be tempted. The very thing I say I will not do usually turns out to be the thing that I do.

We have the privilege and the joy of bearing one another's burdens. We can give all our burdens of life to the Lord. But very often He uses other Christians to help us in bearing them. When you are bearing burdens, you are really sharing blessings. A Christian is not a burden to another Christian. Would a loving mother ever say that her dear child is a burden? Of course not.

Our Lord Jesus Christ has set the example. How many different burdens He helped to carry when He was ministering here on earth! What should we do? We should *restore*—that's a part of bearing one another's burdens. Why should we do it? *Because of love.* How should we do it? *In the spirit of meekness,* not with vainglory or pride.

I wonder if there is somebody whose burden you need to share. As you share another's burdens, God helps you with your own. I've learned that. In the pastoral ministry, as I have shared burdens with people, how good the Lord has been to help me with my own burdens. "Bear ye one another's burdens, and so fulfil the law of Christ" (v. 2).

51

Christians who care are Christians who bear one another's burdens.

Chapter 7

Serve One Another

Caring Christians serve one another.

"For, brethren, ye have been called unto liberty; only use not liberty for an occasion to the flesh, but by love serve one another. For all the law is fulfilled in one word, even in this; Thou shalt love thy neighbour as thyself. But if ye bite and devour one another, take heed that ye be not consumed one of another" (Gal. 5:13-15).

At the end of Galatians 5 we read: "If we live in the Spirit, let us also walk in the Spirit. Let us not be desirous of vain glory, provoking one another, envying one another" (vv. 25,26). In these verses the little phrase "one another" is used a number of times. We can devour one another, we can be consumed one of another, we can provoke one another, we can envy one another. You say, "Well, that doesn't sound like Christian people." No, it doesn't. But Paul was writing to people who had made a profession of faith in Jesus Christ. And in Galatians 5 he was telling them that they should live as those who are free in the Spirit. Verse 16 says, "This I say then, Walk in the Spirit, and ye shall not fulfil the lust of the flesh."

Two Attitudes

There are many references to the Holy Spirit in Galatians. The Holy Spirit of God enables us to serve one another. "By love serve one another" (Gal. 5:13). Paul was contrasting two attitudes. These two attitudes result in two different actions in life. One is the fleshly attitude that regards others as a threat. The other is the spiritual attitude that believes I should be a servant to others.

By nature the flesh is not interested in serving. The flesh is selfish. This old nature that we have fights against the Holy Spirit. "For the flesh lusteth against the Spirit, and the Spirit against the flesh: and these are contrary the one to the other: so that ye cannot do the things that ye would" (v. 17). The Word tells us that a battle is going on in my life and in your life between the flesh and the Spirit. If I yield to the flesh, then the flesh is going to control my life, and this will be seen in the way I treat others. If I yield to the Spirit, then the Holy Spirit is going to control my life, and it will be obvious by the way I treat other people.

It's really quite simple, isn't it? Either the flesh—the old nature—controls us, and we provoke one another, envy one another, devour one another and are consumed of one another; or the Holy Spirit controls us, and by love we serve one another.

The Galatian believers were invaded by a group of false teachers—we call them the Judaizers. Their theology was that you had to obey the Law in order to be a good Christian. I want to make it very clear that Paul was not lawless. He wrote in verse 18: "If ye be led of the Spirit, ye are not under the law."

In Romans 6,7 and 8, Paul dealt with our relationship to the Law. The old nature knows no law. There never was a law given that could change or control the old nature. The new nature needs no law. In Galatians 5:22, Paul said, "But the fruit of the Spirit is love." No law ever given could produce love. "Joy, peace, longsuffering, gentleness, goodness, faith, meekness, temperance [self-control]: against such there is no law" (vv. 22,23). The old nature *knows* no law; the new nature *needs* no law.

How could you pass a law to produce fruit? Suppose your orchard is not bearing, or suppose your garden is not producing. So you go to the city council or the state legislature and say, "Will you please pass a law that would produce fruit?" Of course, they would laugh at you. You don't pass laws to produce fruit. Fruit does not come from law; *fruit comes from life.* This is where legalism is all wrong. Legalistic people who say that you must obey this rule or that law in order to be spiritual are contradicting the Word of God.

Legalism, License or Love

Once again, a Christian is not lawless. This is what Paul said in Galatians 5:13: "For, brethren, ye have been called unto liberty; only use not liberty for an occasion to the flesh." We are facing, then, three possibilities: legalism, license or love.

Legalism means you live under the Law—the Law is your master. This philosophy is seen to be wrong in Galatians. Paul said in Galatians 5:1, "Stand fast therefore in the liberty wherewith Christ hath made us free." We have been set free from the bondage of the Law.

Then someone may say, "I can do what I please!" No, that's the other extreme. Legalism is the one extreme; license is the other extreme. Paul said, "Use not liberty for an occasion to the flesh" (v. 13). License is throwing off all restraint, but liberty means walking in the power of the Holy Spirit.

Freedom is a wonderful thing. Freedom turned *upward* means God is glorified. Freedom turned *outward* means I can serve you. But when freedom is turned *inward,* it becomes license, and this leads to bondage. So one extreme is legalism. Paul said no to legalism. The other extreme is license. Paul said no to license.

The Law of Love

Then what was Paul affirming? Love—the law of love. "For all the law is fulfilled in one word, even in this; Thou shalt love thy neighbour as thyself" (Gal. 5:14). We have encountered this truth over and over again in our study of the "one another" statements in the New Testament. "By love serve one another" (v. 13).

When you look at Galatians 5:15 and Galatians

56

5:26, you don't see much love, do you? The people were biting and devouring one another. How were they doing that? By competition. The Judaizers said, "If you'll obey the Law, then you'll be spiritual." The minute you have rules and regulations to obey, then you can start measuring yourself. And when you start measuring yourself, you can also start measuring other people. We have four children, and each of them is different. It's impossible to measure one by the other. We can't say to the second child, "Well, you ought to be like your big brother." We can't say to the fourth child, "You ought to be like your sister." Each of them is different.

Christians today tend to compare themselves with each other. That's legalism. We tend to measure spirituality quantitatively instead of qualitatively. And this is dangerous. You cannot measure spirituality quantitatively any more than you can measure children quantitatively instead of qualitatively. The fact that one child is a foot taller than another child does not mean he is better than the other child. It just means he's taller, that's all.

There was a tendency among the Galatians to bite and devour one another; there was a tendency to provoke one another and to envy one another. This is the old problem of competition—who is the most spiritual? It is the flesh versus the Spirit. It is self versus others. It is legalism or license versus true liberty in love. Where there is love, there can be freedom. The most liberating thing in all the world is love through the Holy Spirit.

57

When you love others, you don't want to exploit them, bite them or devour them. According to verse 15, if we fight each other, we end up destroying each other. Some groups establish very rigid, legalistic rules, and they say, "Now we are going to be spiritual." Unfortunately, that doesn't happen because "the law of the Spirit of life in Christ Jesus" is the law that ought to run our lives (Rom. 8:2). The Holy Spirit of God, working *in* us and *through* us in love enables us to "serve one another" (Gal. 5:13).

Our Lord Jesus Christ is the greatest example of this. The Pharisees criticized Him because He did not keep their legalistic rules. He did not stop His disciples when they took the grain in the fields (see Matt. 12:1-8). This was perfectly all right according to the Jewish regulations, but they had violated the Sabbath. Our Lord protected them. Our Lord deliberately healed people on the Sabbath Day (see vv. 9-14). The Pharisees were incensed over this! But our Lord Jesus served others in love.

Unless there is love, there will not be true service. Real service has to come from love. In Ephesians 6:6 Paul told the Christian slaves, "Doing the will of God from the heart." They were not just to do God's will out of a sense of duty, but they were to do the will of God *from the heart.* We are to serve in love because we delight in doing it, not because we have to do it. This raises the question, Is my life governed by love? "But by love serve one another" (Gal. 5:13).

"Called Unto Liberty"

This is why we have been "called unto liberty" (Gal. 5:13). We have not been called to liberty so we can sit and enjoy it ourselves. Liberty is too precious for that. Do you know that your liberty in Jesus Christ cost Him His life on the cross? Liberty is a costly thing, whether it be political freedom or whether it be our spiritual freedom. This liberty is so expensive it should not be abused. Why did God call us to liberty? That we might use that liberty to serve one another.

This is a mark of maturity. Mature people do not use their freedom selfishly. They use it for others. We would be wise to yield to the Holy Spirit of God and allow Him to produce the fruit of the Spirit in our lives. The first quality on that list is love: "The fruit of the Spirit is love" (v. 22). I believe that fullness of love produces joy; fullness of love and joy will produce peace; fullness of love, joy and peace will produce longsuffering, and this will produce gentleness. One quality leads to the next one! There is no need for laws, no need for rules and regulations, because we are walking in the Spirit.

Are we filled with vainglory—comparing, contrasting, measuring, making the other person look bad that we might look good? Are we provoking people? Are we envying people? Do we bite and devour? These are marks of fleshly legalism. They are the result of using liberty in the wrong way. How much better it would be if we would just yield to the Holy Spirit and find freedom in the law of love—not the Law of Moses but the law of love that fulfills all of the Law. "By love serve one another" (v. 13).

May the Lord help each of us to be servants—servants, not of sin but of God's people—loving one another, serving one another.

Christians who care serve one another.

Chapter 8

Forgive One Another

Christians who care forgive one another.

Ephesians 4:32 says, "And be ye kind one to another, tenderhearted, forgiving one another, even as God for Christ's sake hath forgiven you."

An unforgiving spirit creates all kinds of problems. In my pastoral ministry, I have counseled some who have had physical difficulties, not because of sickness, not because of injury but because of attitudes in their hearts. Many psychiatrists have observed that people who have emotional problems often have an unforgiving spirit. This is why the Holy Spirit directed Paul to write in Ephesians 4:30-32: "And grieve not the holy Spirit of God, whereby ye are sealed unto the day of redemption. Let all bitterness, and wrath, and anger, and clamour, and evil speaking, be put away from you, with all malice: and be ye kind one to another, tenderhearted, forgiving one another, even as God for Christ's sake hath forgiven you."

Let's try to answer a few questions about this matter of family forgiveness. Remember, Paul was not talking about God's forgiving us for salvation; he was talking about family members forgiving one another—those in the church family who need to forgive each other.

Evidences of an Unforgiving Spirit

What are the evidences of an unforgiving spirit?

Corrupt Communication

I think the greatest evidence is the way we talk about people. In this passage Paul had a great deal to say about speech. For example, he said in Ephesians 4:29, "Let no corrupt communication proceed out of your mouth, but that which is good to the use of edifying [building up], that it may minister grace unto the hearers."

When we have an unforgiving spirit, we say things about people that we shouldn't say. Have you noticed that too? In verse 31 Paul talked about "evil speaking." If I am the kind of person who immediately jumps at the chance to say something evil about a person, that means I am holding a grudge against him. I think one of the first evidences of an unforgiving spirit is what we say about people. If we cannot say something good, it may mean that we have something bad in our hearts.

Inner Feelings

I think another evidence is bad feelings on the inside. Sometimes we are able to control our tongues; sometimes we are able to just bite our lips and not say something evil about somebody. But people would be shocked if they could see what we feel in our hearts! In Ephesians 4:31 Paul talked about bitterness. Somebody hurts us, and we get bitter. Bitterness is to the heart what an infection is to the body.

One summer when I was just a young boy, I was plagued with boils. How they did hurt! What that infection was to my body, bitterness is to my heart. Some Christians hold things inside, and the bitterness just grows like poison in the system. As you well know, when you have an infection, everything is very sensitive, everything hurts. Bitterness is an evidence of an unforgiving spirit. Wrath, anger, clamor—these are the outward evidences of that inward feeling. When there is a fever in the body, it is awfully hard to hide it. And when there is bitterness in the heart, you can't hide it. When that person we are bitter toward is mentioned, we get angry, or we decide to say something that we shouldn't say.

So corrupt communication, evil speaking, bitterness, wrath, anger and malice are evidences of an unforgiving spirit. Malice is that hateful feeling that we nurture down inside. How easy it is to lie in bed at night and to think up all sorts of evil things about those who have wronged us! That is another evidence of an unforgiving spirit.

When we have this kind of attitude, are we hurting the other person? Of course not! If someone has sinned against me or if someone has done something I didn't like and if I harbor resentment down inside, am I hurting that person? No, I am only hurting myself. Having an unforgiving spirit is something like committing spiritual suicide—you are only hurting yourself.

A lady came to me one day and said, "Pastor Wiersbe, I want to apologize to you." I said, "For what?" "Well," she said, "I've had some terrible attitudes toward you." I said, "Now look, that's between you and God. It didn't hurt me, it hurt you." If she had done something outwardly—if she had gone around criticizing me—that would have been a different story. But she had these feelings down inside, and she was not hurting me one bit— she was only hurting herself.

What are the evidences of an unforgiving spirit? Unkind words, evil words, bitter thoughts, bitter feelings down inside.

Essentials for a Forgiving Spirit

What are the essentials for a forgiving spirit? I don't think any of us wants to be unforgiving. We want others to forgive us; therefore, we should forgive others. The person who will not forgive others is destroying the bridge on which he may have to walk himself someday. If we do not forgive others, we are putting a barrier between us and other people and between us and God. In fact, our Lord Jesus said that forgiving our brother is one of the conditions for answered prayer (see Matt. 6:15).

Kindness

One essential for a forgiving spirit is *kindness*. "Be ye kind one to another" (Eph. 4:32). In Ephesians

2:7 Paul had talked about kindness with reference to our salvation: "In the ages to come he [God] might shew the exceeding riches of his grace in his kindness toward us through Christ Jesus." Have you ever stopped to think about how kind God has been to you? Titus 3 describes what we used to be like before we were saved: "For we ourselves also were sometimes [once] foolish, disobedient, deceived, serving divers [various] lusts and pleasures, living in malice and envy, hateful, and hating one another" (v. 3). And if we had stayed like that, we would have been condemned forever. The following verses say, "But after that the kindness and love of God our Saviour toward man appeared, not by works of righteousness which we have done, but according to his mercy he saved us" (vv. 4,5). Why were we able to trust God for salvation? Because of His mercy and kindness.

In II Samuel 9 is a beautiful illustration of the kindness of God. David was reigning as the king, and one day he said, "Is there yet any that is left of the house of Saul, that I may shew him kindness for Jonathan's sake? . . . Is there not yet any of the house of Saul, that I may shew the kindness of God unto him?" (vv. 1,3). What is "the kindness of God"? *Undeserved* kindness. Had Saul done anything good for David? No, yet David said, "I want to show God's kindness to somebody in the house of Saul. I want to forgive." They found Mephibosheth, a lame man who was the son of Jonathan, and David showed kindness to Mephibosheth because of Jonathan. That is the kindness of God.

65

God is kind to us, not because we are so good but for Jesus' sake—because of the grace of the Lord Jesus Christ. If I am going to forgive, I must show kindness. The kindness of God is shown to those who do not deserve it.

Tenderheartedness

Second, I must be *tenderhearted*. A hard heart is a terrible thing. When you have a hard heart, it robs you of blessing and joy. A hard heart is the result of bitterness and anger, wrath and malice. A hard heart results when we harbor evil feelings inside. Paul said that if we are tenderhearted, then we can forgive (see Eph. 4:32).

Honesty

I think a third essential for a forgiving spirit is *honesty*. In Ephesians 4:15 Paul said, "But speaking the truth in love." In Matthew 18 our Lord gave us instructions on how to get along with each other. He said, "If your brother sins against you, go and tell him privately. Don't make a big scene. If he won't listen to you, take one or two others along to help you. And if he won't listen to them, then you can take it to the church" (see vv. 15-17). My experience as a pastor has been that when we take that first step, God usually works in the person's heart, and the problem gets solved.

It's wonderful when saints can be honest with each other in love. Do not harbor bitterness down inside. If someone in your church fellowship has done something against you, don't go around talking about it, don't be bitter, and don't develop a hard heart. Don't think up unkind things to say and do. Go to that person honestly and humbly, and try to get it settled. Do you know why? Because "God for Christ's sake hath forgiven you" (Eph. 4:32).

At the end of Matthew 18 our Lord told the parable about the servant who owed the king a great deal of money. The king ordered him and his family to be sold so that the debt could be paid. But the man begged and said, "Please give me time." And the king took pity on him and forgave him the entire debt. Then the servant met a friend who owed him a small amount of money. He grabbed him by the throat and shook him and said, "Pay what you owe me!" And the man begged him to be patient, saying, "I'll pay if you'll give me time." But he would not give him time, he would not forgive him. When the king heard about this, he was very angry, and he put the servant into prison because he had not forgiven his fellow servant.

Do you know that an unforgiving spirit will put you into an emotional prison? If you have an unforgiving spirit, if you do not forgive your brother or your sister, it will make a prisoner out of you—a prisoner of bitterness and anger, a prisoner of malice. That is such an agonizing way to live! The freedom of forgiveness is a marvelous thing. God has forgiven us, and so we are free from our sins. We forgive others; therefore, we are free in our relationships with one another. And why do we forgive others? Because God has forgiven us.

You may say, "Well, I can forgive, but I can't forget." The Bible does not say that we forget all of these things. In the Bible "to forget" means "not to hold against a person." When God says, "Their sins and their iniquities will I remember no more" (Heb. 8:12), it does not mean He actually forgets. God cannot forget anything. It simply means He does not hold it against us any longer.

I remember evil things that people have done against me, but the pain is gone and the bitterness is gone. I have forgiven them, and I don't hold it against them anymore. You and I can forgive because God has forgiven us.

You may say, "It's awfully hard to forgive." But it's harder *not* to forgive! If we don't forgive, we grieve the Holy Spirit. If we don't forgive, we deny what Jesus did for us on the cross. If we don't forgive, we are not walking in love. Ephesians 5:2 says, "And walk in love, as Christ also hath loved us."

Caring Christians forgive one another. Life is too short to have enemies. Enemies are very expensive. And so we are not going to have enemies; we are going to forgive. We are going to forgive, not because anybody deserves it but for Jesus' sake.

Christians who care forgive one another.

Chapter 9

Submit to One Another

Christians who care submit themselves to one another.

"Submitting yourselves one to another in the fear of God" (Eph. 5:21). "Likewise, ye younger, submit yourselves unto the elder. Yea, all of you be subject one to another, and be clothed with humility: for God resisteth the proud, and giveth grace to the humble" (I Pet. 5:5).

We are living in an era of self-expression and independence. The slogan of most people seems to be, "I'm going to do *my* thing *my* way." Yet the Word of God tells us that the way to fulfillment is through *submission*. This submission is the result of the fullness of the Spirit. "And be not drunk with wine, wherein is excess; but be filled with the Spirit" (Eph. 5:18). How can you tell if someone is filled with the Holy Spirit? Is he going to perform miracles? Will there be some strange glow around his face?

According to Paul, there are three evidences of the fullness of the Holy Spirit. *We are joyful.* "Speaking to yourselves in psalms and hymns and spiritual songs, singing and making melody in your heart to the Lord" (v. 19). *We are thankful.* "Giving thanks always for all things unto God and the Father in the name of our Lord Jesus Christ" (v. 20).

We are submitted to one another. "Submitting yourselves one to another in the fear of God" (v. 21). This whole matter of submission, then, relates to the fullness of the Holy Spirit.

If you and I are walking in the power of the flesh, we will not submit. The flesh is proud, and the flesh always wants to assert itself. The New Testament has nothing good to say about the flesh. "The flesh profiteth nothing" (John 6:63). If we are walking in the Holy Spirit's power, then we are going to be joyful, thankful and submissive.

Please do not reverse that order! We first submit to the Holy Spirit and let Him fill us. To be filled with the Holy Spirit means to be controlled by the Holy Spirit. The Holy Spirit thinks through our minds, He loves through our hearts, He acts through our wills, using the members of our bodies. To be filled with the Spirit means to be controlled by the Spirit. The result of that filling is that we are joyful, thankful and submissive.

When a person is joyful, he has no problem submitting. When he is thankful, he has no problem submitting. But when we are complaining, when we are criticizing, when we think we have gotten a raw deal, then we have a hard time submitting. Then we start asserting ourselves to get what we think we really deserve.

When we mention submission, we are not talking about subjugation or slavery. We are not talking about bondage. In the local church or in the home, there should be no slavery or bondage. We have been called into gracious, wonderful liberty. However, this liberty means freedom to submit to one another.

Perhaps a good illustration is the human body. My body is made up of many different members. Each member has a function to perform, but each member depends upon the other members. As the members of my body submit to one another, the body functions normally. I feel good, and I get my work done. But suppose one member of my body decides not to submit—it wants to go its own way. Then I have trouble! I may have to go to the doctor, and I might even need surgery to correct what is wrong.

We want to apply this principle of submission in three different areas of life. First, consider *our submission to God*. This you find in Ephesians 5:24: "Therefore as the church is subject unto Christ." Second, consider *our submission in the home*. Ephesians 5:22 says, "Wives, submit yourselves unto your own husbands, as unto the Lord." Verse 25 says, "Husbands, love your wives, even as Christ also loved the church, and gave himself for it." Finally, consider *our submission in the church*. Ephesians 5:21 says, "Submitting yourselves one to another in the fear of God."

Submission to God

It all begins with submission to the Lord. "Therefore as the church is subject unto Christ" (Eph. 5:24). The Church must be subject to Christ because Christ is the head of the Church. The

71

Church is not permitted to go its own way. We must be personally submitted to the Lord. The classic text on that is Romans 12:1,2: "I beseech you therefore, brethren, by the mercies of God, that ye present your bodies a living sacrifice, holy, acceptable unto God, which is your reasonable service. And be not conformed to this world: but be ye transformed by the renewing of your mind, that ye may prove what is that good, and acceptable, and perfect, will of God."

What does it mean to submit to the Lord? It means to give Him your body. He wants your body. He has made our bodies His temple. He also wants our minds. The Word commands us not to be conformed to this world but to be transformed. He also wants our wills: "That ye may prove what is that good, and acceptable, and perfect, will of God" (v. 2).

If you want to practice submission, I suggest that every morning you give God your body, your mind and your will. Ask the Holy Spirit to fill you. That is the beginning of a life of daily victory. First, we must submit ourselves to God.

Submission in the Home

Second, we must submit ourselves in the home. Each of us has some home relationship, whether we are single or married. It is too bad that many homes are being destroyed today. It is too bad that Satan is permitted to use destructive forces against the home. I fear one of these destructive forces is selfish independence. "I am going to go *my way!*"

As a pastor, I have seen homes destroyed. It usually happens this way. A home is founded, and the couple makes loving promises to each other and to the Lord. They promise to love, honor, obey and submit. Then somewhere along the line, one of the partners decides he or she wants to go an independent way. The slogan today is "I'm going to do it my way!" One of the partners then goes off and tries to make it alone—breaking vows to God and breaking vows to the other partner.

If there is going to be happiness and holiness in the home, there has to be submission. This is not subjugation, not slavery, not bondage, not lordship but headship—a living, loving relationship. The partners must submit to one another. If a husband is submitted to the Lord and a wife is submitted to the Lord, they have no problem submitting to each other. The wife shows her submission by her obedience, and the husband shows his submission by his love.

Someone has said, "Why didn't Paul say something about the husband's submitting?" He did not use the word "submit," but in Ephesians 5:25 he said that the husband has a great responsibility—he is supposed to love his wife "as Christ also loved the church." That's submission! Christ gave Himself for the Church. The husband's love is to be a sacrificial love. He is to sacrifice so that his wife might be able to submit and obey.

Where this commandment is obeyed and this principle is followed, the home experiences the blessing of God. Once again, it is not slavery, it is

73

not subjugation or bondage. It is the freedom that comes from submitting to the Lord and lovingly submitting to each other. A wife has no problem submitting to a husband who is filled with the Holy Spirit—who is joyful, thankful and submitted to the Lord.

Submission in the Local Church

The third area of submission is in the local church. As a pastor I have had many experiences in churches. As an itinerant Bible teacher it has been my privilege to teach the Word of God in hundreds of churches in many parts of the world. It's a great joy to find a church where people are submitted to one another. Too often, however, people in churches debate with one another and disagree and fight with one another. Some churches split, and the splits produce splinters, and their testimony for the Lord is hurt.

The principle of submission in the church is described in I Peter 5: "Feed [shepherd] the flock of God which is among you, taking the oversight thereof, not by constraint, but willingly; not for filthy lucre, but of a ready mind; neither as being lords over God's heritage, but being ensamples to the flock" (vv. 2,3). There is no place in the church for a dictator. "Likewise, ye younger, submit yourselves unto the elder. Yea, all of you be subject one to another, and be clothed with humility" (v. 5). That phrase reminds me of John 13 where the Lord Jesus put on the towel and washed the disciples'

74

feet. "Be clothed with humility" (I Pet. 5:5). Why? "For God resisteth the proud, and giveth grace to the humble" (v. 5).

It is too bad that we have some sanctified obstructionists on church committees who always have to have their own way. It's too bad that some cannot submit, particularly in matters that are simply not that important. They have to have their own way. Submission in the local church is the way to grow. It is the way for God's blessing to come. It is the way for the Holy Spirit to fill and to work—where the elder and the younger are submitted to the Lord and to each other, where leaders and followers, pastors and people are submitted to the Lord and to one another.

Let me explain why submission is so important. It is important because then *God* controls our lives. If we do not submit, then *other people* control our lives.

The person who says, "I'm going to do it my way! I'll never submit!" actually spends all of his time responding and reacting to the resistance of other people. He thinks he is controlling his life, but he is not—other people are controlling his life. When we submit, God controls; when we don't submit, then other people control. When we refuse to submit, we lead a life of misery and fighting and defensiveness. That's not the kind of life God wants us to live.

"Submitting yourselves one to another in the fear of God" (Eph. 5:21). Are you a submissive Christian? Submissiveness does not mean we *lose* ourselves; it means we *find* ourselves. Submissiveness does not mean that God is going to *cheat* us; it means God is going to *enrich* us.

Christians who care submit to one another in the fear of God.

Chapter 10

Prefer One Another

Christians who care prefer one another in honor. "Let love be without dissimulation [hypocrisy]. Abhor that which is evil; cleave [cling] to that which is good. Be kindly affectioned one to another with brotherly love; in honour preferring one another" (Rom. 12:9,10). You can reverse that sentence and make it read: "Preferring one another in honor."

Everyone likes to receive recognition. Something in us likes to be appreciated. Certainly nothing is wrong with honest recognition. In fact, Paul wrote to the Thessalonians and told them to know their spiritual leaders and respect them, to honor them for the work they had done (I Thess. 5:12,13). There is certainly nothing wrong with honest recognition. God gets the glory, but God's servants deserve honor.

But the admonition of Romans 12:9,10 tells us that we should prefer one another in honor. That simply means you and I should be willing for others to get the recognition and to receive the honor. It means that we should be willing to not be recognized at all if this is the will of God. Christians are to prefer one another in honor.

I want to look at this statement from two different directions—first of all, what it does *not* mean and, second, what it *does* mean and how we can practice it.

What Preferring One Another Does Not Mean

First of all, *what does this not mean?* "In honour preferring one another" (Rom. 12:10).

Not Empty Flattery

It does not mean empty flattery. Books are available these days that tell you how to flatter your way into or out of anything. There is a brand of psychology that tells you to find "the hot button" in every person's life—find out what they are really interested in—and then you can use that to your own advantage. This leads, of course, to manipulating people. Paul was not talking about empty flattery because in Romans 12:9 he said, "Let love be without dissimulation [hypocrisy]."

There is a hypocritical kind of love. There is a shallow, gushy kind of love that is all words and no deeds. There is a kind of love that is manufactured, artificial, brittle and does not last. Paul was telling us that our love for one another should be sincere and honest. There should be no hypocrisy involved in it. Flattery is something that Christians must flee.

Paul wrote in I Thessalonians 2:5,6: "For neither at any time used we flattering words, as ye know, nor a cloke [cloak] of covetousness; God is witness: nor of men sought we glory, neither of you, nor yet of others, when we might have been burdensome,

78

as the apostles of Christ." Paul did not flatter people into the kingdom. Paul did not flatter people to get something out of them. He did not manipulate people.

Some preaching I listen to is very manipulative. It is flattery, and God cannot bless that kind of ministry. In fact, God warned against flattering lips: "A lying tongue hateth those that are afflicted by it; and a flattering mouth worketh ruin" (Prov. 26:28). God hates flattery. So "in honour preferring one another" does not mean that we go around flattering each other.

Not Belittling Ourselves

Second, *it does not mean that we belittle ourselves.* Sometimes people have the idea that "in honour preferring one another" (Rom. 12:10) means that we have to lie about ourselves and belittle ourselves. These people go around saying, "I can't do anything" or "I'm not worth anything." That, of course, is sin. We are worth something. Every believer has spiritual gifts that God has given to him. Romans 12:3 says, "For I say, through the grace given unto me, to every man that is among you, not to think of himself more highly than he ought to think; but to think soberly, according as God hath dealt to every man the measure of faith." We want to avoid two extremes: We should not think *too highly* of ourselves, and we must not think *too lowly* of ourselves.

When God called Moses, Moses belittled himself.

79

Moses said, "I am not an eloquent speaker. I am slow of speech" (see Ex. 4:10). God had to rebuke him and say, "I made your tongue, I made your mouth. Now you obey Me!" (see vv. 11,12). Belittling yourself is belittling God. Some people go to God's house and say, "Well, I'm not very important. I don't teach a Sunday school class, I'm not on the board, I don't sing in the choir, so I'm not very important." But you are important—each believer is important to God.

In Romans 12:4-8 Paul talked about the members of the Body. "For as we have many members in one body, and all members have not the same office: so we, being many, are one body in Christ, and every one members one of another" (vv. 4,5). So if you belittle yourself, you are belittling the other members of the Body because we belong to each other. "Having then gifts differing according to the grace that is given to us" (v. 6). Then he listed the different gifts that we are to use as God has apportioned them to us. We should not belittle ourselves; neither should we overestimate ourselves. Rather, we should wisely use the gift God has given to us.

If someone says to you, "We need your help in Vacation Bible School" or "We need your help in the summer camp program" and if you are able to help, you should do so. But if you say, "No, I can't do anything," that really is not humility—that is pride. You are wanting them to say, "But you can. We know what a good worker you are." "In honour preferring one another" (Rom. 12:10) does not mean empty flattery, and it does not mean belittling

80

yourself. You had better admit what gifts God has given to you and use them to the glory of God. That is the humble thing to do.

Third, *it does not mean showing partiality.* We all tend to show partiality. Leaders have a tendency to like certain people and to get along better with certain people. We have to be very careful about this. When Paul wrote to Timothy to instruct him about the local church, he said, "I charge thee before God, and the Lord Jesus Christ, and the elect angels, that thou observe these things without preferring one before another, doing nothing by partiality" (I Tim. 5:21). "Preferring one before another" is showing prejudice—prejudice against somebody else. Paul was admonishing this young pastor not to show partiality.

This is a hard principle to practice—it really is. I have pastored three churches, and I know that some people are very cooperative and some are not. It's so easy to be partial. But we are not to show partiality. "In honour preferring one another" (Rom. 12:10) does not mean that we prefer one and hurt another. It does not mean that we become so wrapped up in one person that we neglect another.

What Preferring One Another Means

"In honour preferring one another" (Rom. 12:10) simply means putting other people ahead of our-

81

selves. That's so easy to say and so hard to do!

This was one of the problems in the church at Philippi. Paul wrote to them in Philippians 2: "Let nothing be done through strife or vainglory; but in lowliness of mind let each esteem other better than themselves" (v. 3). That word "better" means "more important." Let each esteem the other person more important than himself. Other people have greater talents than I do in certain areas. I'm not a good athlete, I'm not a mechanic, I'm not a cook, I'm not a painter, and I can't fix things. I have to admit that other people are better in those areas. But that is not what Paul was talking about. Paul was saying we must recognize our own gifts and abilities, but we must put others *ahead of ourselves*.

Someone has said that the way to have joy is to put *Jesus* first, *others* second and *yourself* last; and that spells J-O-Y. This is true. "In honour preferring one another" (Rom. 12:10).

This attitude demands love. This is why Paul wrote in Romans 12:10: "Be kindly affectioned one to another with brotherly love; in honour preferring one another." When you love someone, you want that person to be in the place of honor.

Consider the story of Abraham and Lot (Gen. 13). Their flocks and herds had multiplied, there had been a famine in the land, and consequently there wasn't enough pasture for both of them. Fighting was taking place among the herdsmen. Abraham could have said, "Now, Lot, I am older than you are; I am in charge. Therefore, I suggest you go here or you go there." He did not say that.

Abraham said, "Now, Lot, if you go to the left, I'll go to the right; if you go to the right, I'll go to the left" (see v. 9). He preferred to give the honor to Lot. Lot abused that privilege, but that wasn't Abraham's fault. Abraham showed the right spirit—"in honour preferring one another" (Rom. 12:10).

This is where King Saul got into trouble. God began to use David as a warrior. And when the soldiers came back, the women sang, "Saul hath slain his thousands, and David his ten thousands" (I Sam. 18:7). And what happened? Saul got envious and jealous. Instead of saying, "Praise God for this warrior!" and preferring David and giving him honor, Saul became envious. He began to watch David, and before long envy turned to hatred—he tried to kill David! (see vv. 8-11). It is very important that you and I have a right relationship to other believers. We should give honor where honor is due. We should show respect where respect is due. And most of all, we should do so to the glory of Jesus Christ.

Let's make this very practical. I have been in church services where people have stopped the pastor and said, "Why did you announce this Sunday school class meeting and didn't announce ours?" And the poor pastor was caught between two Sunday school classes. I have been in places where a name was left out of the bulletin, and as a result, someone lost his joy that day. If, in our local churches, we would just pray, "O God, help me to get my work done, and it makes no difference who gets the honor, as long as You get the glory," what a

83

difference it would make. Whenever you find a church family where people are looking for recognition and praise, you have problems, division and dissension. We should be like John the Baptist, who said, "This my joy therefore is fulfilled. He must increase, but I must decrease" (John 3:29,30).

So the next time we have the opportunity to let somebody else be first in line, let's do it. The next time we have the opportunity to let some other believer get a little bit of recognition and appreciation, let's encourage it. Let's not sit back and say, "Well, I work harder than he does; somebody should surely recognize me." Instead, let's say, "Thank You, Father, for this fellow Christian. Thank You for the hard work that he does, and I pray that You will bless him abundantly." May there not be in our hearts that terrible poison of envy, strife, jealousy and competition. Rather, may we practice what Paul instructed in Romans 12:10: "In honour preferring one another."

Christians who care don't go around promoting themselves. Christians who care prefer one another in honor.

Chapter 11

Show Hospitality to One Another

Christians who care show hospitality to one another without grudging.

"But the end of all things is at hand: be ye therefore sober, and watch unto prayer. And above all things have fervent charity [love] among yourselves: for charity [love] shall cover the multitude of sins. Use hospitality one to another without grudging. As every man hath received the gift, even so minister the same one to another, as good stewards of the manifold grace of God" (I Pet. 4:7-10).

So often we forget that hospitality is a gift from God. Notice in I Peter 4 that Peter connected hospitality in verse 9 with ministry in verse 10. Christian hospitality is a gift.

In my own ministry, it has been my privilege to travel to many places. How I thank God for people who have the gift of Christian hospitality! Our Lord Jesus promised that if we would forsake our homes to serve Him, then He would reward us "an hundredfold" (Matt. 19:29). I have experienced the fulfillment of that promise. I can go so many places where the doors are open to me. I am grateful, too, that my wife and I have had the privilege of experiencing and sharing Christian hospitality in our own home. Our four children have grown up expecting people to be there. We enjoy it, and they have been enriched by it. Of course, we live now in a generation that is more concerned about getting away from home than being at home, and for some reason, we don't have the kind of old-fashioned Christian hospitality that we used to have. May I recommend that you use your home as a place of ministry to serve God. That is why He gave it to you. You don't have that house and furniture and food just for yourself and your family—it's there to share. "Use hospitality one to another without grudging" (I Pet. 4:9).

Hospitality Is an Important Ministry

I want to deal with several facts with reference to this matter of hospitality. The first fact is this: *Hospitality is an important ministry.* We have a tendency to think that the people who preach the gospel and write books and sing are doing the ministry. They are, and we thank God for them. But an important ministry can also be performed in the home.

By the Spiritual Leaders

In I Timothy 3, when Paul gave the qualifications for the bishop, or the pastor, he said, "A bishop then must be blameless, the husband of one wife, vigilant, sober, of good behaviour, given to hospitality, apt to teach; not given to wine, no striker, not greedy of filthy lucre; but patient, not a brawler, not

86

covetous; one that ruleth well his own house, having his children in subjection with all gravity" (vv. 2-4). So hospitality is important to the pastor's ministry. The same admonition is repeated in Titus 1:8. God expects Christian leaders—bishops, pastors, elders—to open their homes for ministry. He also expects that the spiritual leader will use his home for ministry in the way he raises his own children. How sad it is when someone who is seeking to lead the church of God is unable to lead his own household.

By Everyone

So hospitality is an important admonition, not only to the spiritual leaders of the church but also to each member of the church. All of us have the privilege and responsibility of hospitality. "Distributing to the necessity of saints; given to hospitality" (Rom. 12:13). To whom was Paul writing? He was writing to the everyday members of the church—the garden-variety Christians. Not only is the pastor to open his home for hospitality, but so are the church members.

The phrase "given to hospitality" means that it is to be *habitual*. It is not an obligation; it's an opportunity. Believers are to yield themselves to it; they are to become addicted to it, so to speak. They are to open their homes to the glory of God.

The Christian home is to be a heaven on earth. That great Baptist preacher, Charles Haddon Spurgeon, once said, "When home is ruled according to God's word, angels might be asked to stay with us, and they would not find themselves out of their element." Isn't that an interesting statement? I wonder if the angels of God would feel at home in our homes today?

God has established only three institutions in this world—human government, the Church and the home. When God brought Adam and Eve together and performed, as it were, the first marriage ceremony in Eden, He established the first home. So the Christian home is important. It is important to the members of the family, and it is important to others. The admonition to "use hospitality one to another without grudging" (I Pet. 4:9) is important.

One verse we usually think of in terms of hospitality is Hebrews 13:2: "Be not forgetful to entertain strangers: for thereby some have entertained angels unawares." Abraham did that (see Gen. 18:1-22). One day while Abraham was resting, he saw three strangers coming down the road. He did not know who they were. Some of the pictures we see of this scene have halos over the heads of these people, and two of them appear to be angels and one appears to be the Lord Jesus. But those pictures are not accurate. Abraham did not know who the strangers were at first. Later on he found out he was entertaining our Lord and two of His angels. Abraham entertained angels unawares!

The word "angels" in the Greek New Testament means "messengers." The word that we translate "angel" can be translated "messenger." Did you ever stop to think that a guest in your home could be God's messenger? I remember so many times when we have had folks in our home, and they have been messengers of God—they have brought blessing to us.

Let me share just one instance from my own life. When I was in my first pastorate in northern Indiana, we entertained a wonderful Christian pastor who came to our church for a Bible conference. He was with us for about a week and lived right in our home. My wife and I were just a young married couple, and we had an upstairs apartment. It was not very fancy, but our guest made himself right at home. He was like a father to us during those days. Little did I realize how God would use that man in my life. A few years later, he contacted me to see if I might come and unite my ministry with his in the church that he was pastoring. We did, and then, when God called him home, I became pastor of that church. That pastor was a messenger of God in our home, and we have been blessed, and are still being blessed, because of that experience.

To be hospitable is an important admonition for the sake of the people in your home. Your children will be blessed if you are given to hospitality. You say, "Well, we don't have a great deal to offer." That's not the point. Any person who loves God and who comes to your home is happy to be there regardless of what you have to offer. After all, you're not out to impress people, you are out to express the love of God.

Hospitality Was Vital to the Early Church

Second, *hospitality was a vital part of the early church.* Generally speaking, the people were rather poor. Many of them were persecuted as they fled from one place to another, and they had to stay somewhere. And so the Christians opened their homes to one another—to the persecuted saints, to the traveling preachers.

In III John 1:5-8 we have a little glimpse of this: "Beloved, thou doest faithfully whatsoever thou doest to the brethren, and to strangers; which have borne witness of thy charity [love] before the church: whom if thou bring forward on their journey after a godly sort, thou shalt do well: because that for his name's sake they went forth, taking nothing of the Gentiles. We therefore ought to receive such, that we might be fellow-helpers to the truth." John was talking about the traveling preachers and evangelists who were going through town. Gaius, the man who received this letter, opened his home to them, and John said to Gaius, "You are doing a faithful work. You are a fellow-helper to the truth." You and I can help the truth of God to go forth by showing hospitality—by taking care of those who minister.

Of course, the early church assemblies met in the homes. Many times when the service was over, some of the people had no place to go, so they just stayed! Wouldn't that be an interesting experience to have a congregation just stay right with you! Hospitality was a very important part of the early

90

church, and it should be important to Christians today. As times of economic pressure increase, we may find ourselves more and more given to hospitality. People may lose their jobs. People may need some place to stay. A missionary coming home from the field needs a place to stay, and we can provide it. You and I should be given to hospitality.

Hospitality Brings Blessing

Finally, let me remind you that *being given to hospitality brings blessing.* It always does. "Give, and it shall be given unto you" (Luke 6:38). When we open our hearts, our hands and our homes, God always pours out His blessing. He always multiplies His blessing when we share. That is why Peter wrote: "Use hospitality one to another without grudging" (I Pet. 4:9). Don't complain about it! Don't gripe about it! Verse 10 says we are to use what God has given to us "as good stewards of the manifold grace of God." You are a steward of your home—use it for God's glory. You are a steward of the money and the food that God has given to you—use them for God's glory. God always blesses those who are unselfish, who share what they have with others.

One of the remarkable statements of our Lord is in Matthew 25:35,36. I realize there are some prophetic overtones to this section, but there is a practical application as well. "For I was an hungered, and ye gave me meat [food]: I was thirsty, and ye gave me drink: I was a stranger, and ye took me in:

naked, and ye clothed me." The righteous then will answer Him, asking, "Lord, when did we do all of this?" (see vv. 37-39). And He will reply, "Inasmuch as ye have done it unto one of the least of these my brethren, ye have done it unto me" (v. 40). When you and I share our homes and what we have with others, we are doing it for Jesus Christ.

Christians who care show hospitality to one another.

Chapter 12

Lie Not to One Another

Christians who care will not lie to one another.

"Mortify therefore your members which are upon the earth; fornication, uncleanness, inordinate affection, evil concupiscence [desire], and covetousness, which is idolatry: for which things' sake the wrath of God cometh on the children of disobedience: in the which ye also walked some time, when ye lived in them. But now ye also put off all these; anger, wrath, malice, blasphemy, filthy communication out of your mouth. Lie not one to another, seeing that ye have put off the old man with his deeds; and have put on the new man, which is renewed in knowledge after the image of him that created him: where there is neither Greek nor Jew, circumcision nor uncircumcision, Barbarian, Scythian, bond nor free: but Christ is all, and in all" (Col. 3:5-11).

God takes our words seriously. One day believers are going to stand at the Judgment Seat of Christ, and every idle word is going to come up for examination. The ninth commandment says, "Thou shalt not bear false witness" (Ex. 20:16). This same commandment is repeated in Romans 13:9: "Thou shalt not bear false witness." In John 8:44 we are told that Satan is a liar and the father of lies. In

Proverbs 6:16,17 we are told that God hates liars. In fact, in Revelation 21:8,27 and 22:15 God informs us that liars will end up in hell.

God can forgive any sin. We know this. The Apostle Peter did not tell the truth when he denied our Lord, and yet he was forgiven. Often you and I, under some kind of pressure, have succumbed to temptation, and we told what we said was just a half-lie or a half-truth. Then our hearts convicted us, and we confessed it, and God forgave us. But God takes lying seriously. Let's try to answer four questions as we consider this admonition: "Lie not one to another" (Col. 3:9).

What Is a Lie?

What is a lie? I suppose the simplest definition would be that a lie is a deliberate and conscious misrepresentation of the truth. A lie has to be deliberate; it is not an accident. If my watch is not working properly and if you ask me what time it is, I would give you the wrong time—but not deliberately. I am not deliberately trying to misrepresent the truth. Sometimes we fail to tell the truth by accident, and sometimes we are ignorant of the truth. But a lie represents a *deliberate* intent to deceive. Our motive is to deceive.

We can lie just by saying things in a certain way. The inflection of our voice could make people believe that we mean something else. We can lie with our lips, and we can certainly lie with our lives as well. *What* we say and *why* we say it and the *way*

94

we say it determines whether or not our words are true. A lie is a deliberate and conscious misrepresentation of the truth.

Why Do We Lie?

Why do we lie? Wouldn't it be easy just to tell the truth? I think it was Abraham Lincoln who said, "If a man is going to be a liar, he had better have a good memory." There's a great deal to be said for that advice!

Pride

Why do we lie? Sometimes we lie out of *pride*— we want to impress people. In Acts 5 Ananias and Sapphira tried to lie to God and did lie to the church because they wanted to impress people. Barnabas had given a gift to the church, and Ananias and Sapphira thought they would get in on some of the honor, but they lied. I don't know why we think we have to impress people. The only person we really have to please is the Lord.

Fear

Sometimes we lie because of *fear*—we don't want to be discovered. We are hiding something, and we want to escape punishment or trouble. The poet, Sir Walter Scott, has well said, "Oh, what a tangled web we weave, / When first we practice to deceive!" Can you remember when you were just a little child, and you told a lie? Then you had to tell another lie to cover up the first one. Before long you were *really* in trouble. I can remember doing that. We lie because we are afraid.

Hatred

Sometimes we lie out of *hatred*—we want to hurt people. If we tell the truth, it might sound too good, so we make something up just to hurt them.

Unbelief

I think at the bottom of all lying is *unbelief*. We don't really believe that the truth is the best way. Jesus said, "I am . . . the truth" (John 14:6). The Holy Spirit is the Spirit of truth (16:13). God's Word is truth (17:17). God Himself is the God of truth (Deut. 32:4). God will bless the truth.

Sometimes the truth seems to get us into trouble. That's only temporary; ultimately the truth will prevail. When you doubt God's Word and say, "I'd better lie and get out of this," stop! God will bless the truth. We lie because of pride, fear, hatred or unbelief.

To Whom Do We Lie?

To whom do we lie? Of course, we lie *to one another.* This is so easy to do because other people are not able to read our minds and hearts. We lie to one another by *exaggerating.* We have to be very

96

careful not to fall into the trap of exaggeration. Sometimes announcements are exaggerated. Sometimes reports are exaggerated. We might even exaggerate statistics.

Sometimes we *flatter* one another. That's a form of lying. We can even lie while we're singing in church. I wonder how many people have sung, "I'll go where You want me to go, dear Lord, . . . I'll be what You want me to be," and yet in their hearts they have no desire to do anything God wants them to do. It's possible for a soloist or a choir member to lie in church through singing. In one of the churches I was pastoring, a young lady who was out of the will of God was going to sing a solo in the morning service. I asked her, "What are you going to sing?" She told me. It was a song of dedication. I said, "You had better not sing today, because you can't sing that song honestly." She was upset with me, but she knew I was telling the truth. We can lie even *in acts of serving God.*

I could lie in *preaching.* How easy it is to preach and to give people the impression that you are so spiritual, and yet deep down inside God may see something altogether different. We can lie in *praying.* How many people have stood up in a prayer meeting and said, "O Lord, provide what is needed for the missionaries," and yet they have not given one dime to missions!

We can lie *to ourselves.* First John 1 tells us that a progressive degeneration begins when we start lying. First John 1:6 says, "If we say that we have fellowship with him, and walk in darkness, we lie,

97

and do not the truth." We are lying to other people. Verse 8 says, "If we say that we have no sin, we deceive ourselves." Now we are lying to ourselves. Some Christians who are walking in darkness actually believe they are in the light. They have sin in their lives, but they are lying to themselves and convincing themselves that it really is not sin.

Finally, in verse 10 we read: "If we say that we have not sinned, we make him a liar." Now we're *trying to lie to God!* Did you know that you really cannot lie to God? We can try. Ananias and Sapphira tried to lie, but God knew their hearts. God knows the thoughts and the intents of the heart.

And so we lie to one another, and we lie to ourselves, and we try to lie to God.

How Should We Tell the Truth?

How should we tell the truth? We don't ask *why* we should tell the truth—we know *why* we should tell the truth. Because it is God's commandment. We are a new creation; we have put off the old life with its lies. "Lie not one to another, seeing that ye have put off the old man with his deeds; and have put on the new man, which is renewed in knowledge" (Col. 3:9,10). As we grow in grace and in the knowledge of our Lord Jesus Christ, we put off the old, and we put on the new. The new man, the new creation, enjoying newness of life has to practice truth. So we don't ask, "*Why* should we tell the truth?" We know why we should.

98

In Love

The question is, *How* should we tell the truth? To begin with, we should tell the truth *in love*. Ephesians 4:15 says, "But speaking the truth in love." Always speak the truth in love. Don't use the truth as a weapon to hurt somebody. Use the truth as a tool to build somebody.

When I go to the dentist, he is usually very tender and gentle. Occasionally, when he has to do some really deep work, he gives me something to deaden the pain. I appreciate that. In the same way we are to speak the truth in love.

With Grace

Second, we should speak the truth *with grace*. Colossians 4:6 says, "Let your speech be alway with grace, seasoned with salt, that ye may know how ye ought to answer every man." Gracious speech comes from a heart that is filled with the grace of our Lord Jesus Christ—"seasoned with salt." Never say to someone, "Now take this with a grain of salt." *You* put the salt in it! Salt means purity. Salt means it contains no corruption. When we speak to others, we should always speak graciously and with purity.

In Jesus' Name

Finally, when we speak, we should speak *in the name of the Lord Jesus*. Colossians 3:16,17 says,

"Let the word of Christ dwell in you richly in all wisdom; teaching and admonishing one another in psalms and hymns and spiritual songs, singing with grace in your hearts to the Lord. And whatsoever ye do in word or deed, do all in the name of the Lord Jesus, giving thanks to God and the Father by him." If we can't say it in the name of, and to the glory of, the Lord Jesus Christ, then we should not say it at all.

"Lie not one to another" (v. 9). It would be wonderful if all of us would start being honest with God in our praying and in our worship and start being honest with one another. In the committee meeting, in the business meeting, in the worship service and in private conversation we should practice honesty and truthfulness.

Christians who care will not lie to one another.

Back to the Bible is a nonprofit ministry dedicated to Bible teaching, evangelism and edification of Christians worldwide.

If we may assist you in knowing more about Christ and the Christian life, please write to us without obligation:

Back to the Bible
P.O. Box 82808
Lincoln, NE 68501